HANDBOOKS OF EUROPEAN NATIONAL DANCES

EDITED BY
VIOLET ALFORD

DANCES OF BULGARIA

Plate 1
Ovchata from Hlevene

DANCES of BULGARIA

RAINA KATSAROVA

PUBLISHED
UNDER THE AUSPICES OF
THE ROYAL ACADEMY OF DANCING
AND THE
LING PHYSICAL EDUCATION ASSOCIATION

LONDON
MAX PARRISH & COMPANY

TRANSLATED BY
MARGO HADJI MISHEVA
ILLUSTRATED BY
PAMELA WOODS
AFTER DRAWINGS BY
EVGENIYA ILIEVA LEPAVTSOVA
ASSISTANT EDITOR
YVONNE MOYSE

First published in 1951
This edition published in 2021 by
The Noverre Press
Southwold House
Isington Road
Binsted
Hampshire
GU34 4PH

ISBN 978-1-914311-08-6

© 2021 The Noverre Press

CONTENTS

INTRODUCTION	*Page* 7
Horos	7
The Răchenitsa	9
Men's Dances	9
Ritual Dances	10
Women's Dances	13
Music	14
Costume	15
When Dancing May Be Seen	17
Folk Dance Groups	18
THE DANCES	19
Poise of Body and Arm Holds	20
Basic Steps	21
Răchenitsa	24
Tsone, Milo Chedo	30
Temenugo, Temenushke	33
Ovchata	36
BIBLIOGRAPHY	40

Illustrations in Colour, pages 2, 12, 29, 39
Map of Bulgaria, page 6

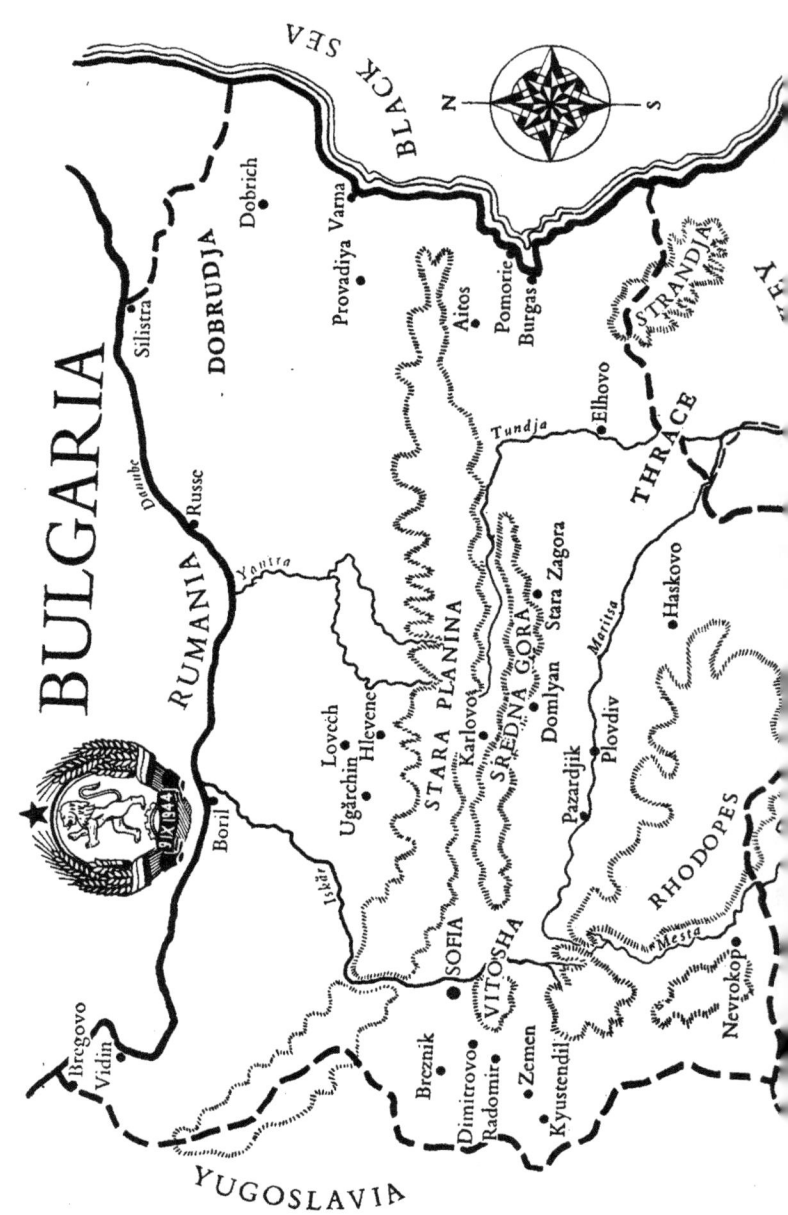

INTRODUCTION

THE wealth of steps and the exceptionally varied rhythms found in Bulgarian folk dance point to a long process of development arising from a series of both ancient and modern cultures. Our dances are, with few exceptions, community dances. Amongst them the Horo, in its circular or Chain form, takes the most important place in village amusements. Horos are danced on Sundays and feast days, so many joining that the Chain has to break up into several lines. Horos are woven into the very ritual of a Bulgarian wedding, into all family and costal gatherings: when girls go to the well for water in the evening the young men will join them in a Horo; during a respite from harvesting Horos will begin in the fields.

At village fairs, held usually on the occasion of a Church festival, the Horo circles will swing from morning to night, one dancer replacing another, one piper following another. A folk song tells of a Horo which went on for three days without stopping. Groups of people coming in to a fair from distant villages try to outdance each other and vie with each other to 'call the tune', which means paying the musicians for a couple of hours. Father or sweetheart will pay for any girl who wants to lead the dance. Everybody and anybody goes into the Chain, taking his place regardless of his poverty or wealth, his station or his lack of it. The Horo is the epitome of democracy.

The peasants of the country region round Sofia, known as *shopi*, have a great reputation as Horo dancers, and the story goes of one of these agile men crying out in the excitement of a Horo, 'Have a care, Mother Earth, it is a *shop* who is treading you!'

Every region has its Horos. In Western Bulgaria they are small-stepped and lively, in the North wilder, in Thrace slower and more solemn; the women will dance in one way and the men in another, marked by virile stamping. The Chain dance is called *vodeno horo*, a led Horo, the long line of people needing a leader. The most typical led Horo the 'crooked' Horo in 11/16. In this the right and left leaders—that is the first and last dancer—wind the Chain to right and to left, into a spiral and out again, all at the same breath-taking tempo. Leader and last man frequently wave their free hand, sometimes a kerchief, while the leader has even been described, in a folk song, as dancing with an open umbrella as insignia of office.*

Another form is *na prât*, 'on a stave', which means a frontal straight line, danced by selected dancers. The names of Horos show their migrations from mountains to plain, brought by harvesters, gypsy musicians, by shepherds, by soldiers. Others seem to show they have come from across the borders—the Serbian, Wallachian, Greek Horo, and so forth. Then there are Sheep, Hare, Prawn and Goose Horos, and others named from some local herb. A very small-stepped quick Horo is 'Lentils', while the Paidushka, because of its halting steps, is called 'The Cripple'.

At a *sedyanka*—when the neighbours come in in the evening to lend a hand with shelling and beating sunflower seed, picking cotton, carding wool or spinning—a certain 'amusement' Horo will be sung and danced. The dancers prolong a syllable for several bars, forming a circle and bowing low towards the centre. The ring is thus brought

* Cf. *Dances of Denmark* in this series, p. 10.

8

up tight, to be opened wide again as all spread their arms and slowly lean backwards.

Our Bulgarian has preserved his style and kept his dance-type pure in spite of the five centuries of Turkish occupation of his country. There is no erotic base in his dance, and in the midst of the liveliest excitement he keeps his dignity.

THE RĂCHENITSA

This is the most lively of our dances and the freest, everyone giving rein to his fancy, his gift of improvisation and his endurance. It is not rare to see a particularly strong performer outlast three who, one after the other, endeavour to dance him down. An admiring circle is formed to encourage him with shouts and rhythmic hand-clapping. The Răchenitsa can begin as a Couple dance and, as more and more join, become a Community dance.

At a wedding bridesmaids and bridegroom's men dance a Răchenitsa at the head of the procession as it leaves the church. Another is danced by the groom's relations when, on the Monday after the ceremony, they visit the bride's mother. On the Monday also, when the bride goes first from her new home to fetch water and to offer her own mother fresh water, young men and girls dance a Răchenitsa in front of her. In the village of Domlyan in the Karlovo district, two puppets of the Punch and Judy type are made to dance a Răchenitsa before bridal processions.

MEN'S DANCES

Certain small-stepped, lively Horos are done by men only. One of these is the straight-line Horo, 'on a stave'. Others must have belonged to certain trades, such as the Masons', the Potters', the Butchers' and the Shepherds' Horo, in which steps and gestures reflect movements used in the work of these trades. Soldiers dance Horos in barracks, seeking to outdance each other in companies, batteries and squadrons.

The Hare dance is a men's dance, miming two hares in the moonlight. The dancers leap like hares, chase each other, jump over each other, turn somersaults and listen intently. Ears are made by flapping hands or by real hare ears fixed to sticks. A huntsman, after some comic mime, kills one of the animals.

'How Black Pepper is Sown' is a wedding dance sung and performed by men, once ritual in intent, now merely for amusement. It requires ten men or more holding hands in a semicircle. They sing, with comic solemnity miming the actions of sowing, gathering, pounding, and threading on strings to dry. Such agricultural dance-games, once of magical meaning, are known all across Europe, the English 'Oats and Beans and Barley O' offering a good example.

RITUAL DANCES

Dancing has a large part in most of our seasonal customs and these customs are not concentrated entirely round Carnival but make up a calendar cycle which, with good foundation, is considered as the remnants of the Dionysian cult.

Dances and masks of the famous Suruvakari in the Breznik district appear on St. Basil's Eve and Day. The fantastic masks are more than six feet high, and are covered at the top with wings, feathers and heads of animals. The wearers, armed with clubs and wooden swords, go from house to house 'leaping for health and good crops'. They face the master of the house and jump madly to the deafening sound of a drum and of the cattle-bells on their belts. Ancient folk characters go with them, the Bride and her Baby and animal-men who, to keep pace with the times, have turned into aeroplanes and into trains with several carriages dragging behind them. When two companies meet they face each other and nowadays dance in a friendly spirit, forgetting the furious fighting in which they used to indulge.

The week preceding Lent sees Kukeri performing their dance-drama. Ten to fifteen men with blackened faces dress up in the women's *sukmani*, woollen over-dresses, and don high masks decorated with feathers, flowers, ribbons and mirrors. They too are armed with clubs and swords, and take Bride and Baby with them and an 'Arab' with duly blackened face. Their musician is a bagpiper, and often a King is chosen who performs the ritual ploughing and sowing. In the Strandja mountains the Kukeri even dance on stilts. Superhuman height may denote ancient divinities or cult heroes—the great ones.

At threshing time in the Elhovo district a 'Camel' goes about at night dancing. This is in reality an immense Hobby-Horse type of creature with a fantastic animal-head very much like the 'Wild Mule' of Catalonia. The Camel leader 'blesses' the house, bestowing fertility, and the farmers give him wheat in return for his good offices.

During Whitsun week Rusalii appear in many Danubian villages. Their dancing is for two purposes: the first round a sick person, for magical healing, the second for general fertility together with the amusement of the onlookers. The name comes from the Latin Rosalia (a word connected with the hanging-up of garlands at the festival of the Rosales Escae), and the present-day dances are distinguished for their rapid tempo, small stamping steps—which are most exhausting—and the play of small staves.

The very ancient fire-dancing is not yet extinct. These Nestinar dances take place on June 3rd, the performers stepping barefoot on live coals to the music of bagpipe and big drum. This is preceded by processions in which sacred icons are carried and Horos in many separate chains are danced to song and bagpipe. These processions, unlike the fire-dancing, are well preserved.

Plate 2   'Tsone, milo chedo'.   Zemen region

WOMEN'S DANCES

Many villages have retained the tradition of sung dances. Women's sung Horos are of a quiet type, and certain of their ritual Horos are slow.

Girls' spring dances are sung; the younger ones perform dance-games with long dialogues in song, two singing on one side, a chorus answering them. The contending sides move forward and back again in the style of many an English singing game. The game ends when the original two have pulled over all the girls on the opposite side.

The Saturday before Palm Sunday, called in Bulgaria St. Lazarus' Day, is the greatest festival of the year for the girls. They form themselves into companies, big or small, to go from house to house singing and dancing, thus 'bringing in the spring' to the village. The girls keep special clothes for this great day and in some districts wear richly decorated head-dresses finished with upstanding bunches of pale, lightly waving grass. Sometimes they are led by an older girl, the Kumitsa or *commère*. Their songs have traditional verses suitable for different occasions and different persons. Everybody can thus be greeted correctly. A newly married couple will hear:

> *For the good health of this house,*
> *For its health and abundance,*
> *Dance for this young bride*
> *And for next year's cradle.*

To a childless woman they sing:

> *Apple-tree, little apple-tree,*
> *Why dost thou blossom*
> *And not bear fruit,*
> *As in the first year,*
> *White and red apples . . .*

While to the cornfields, as the beautifully dressed, colourful little group passes, they sing:

The field we passed,
Exhausting the ground:
From two ears, a basket of corn;
From two grapes a cask of wine!

The girls are welcomed everywhere as harbingers of spring, and receive gifts of money, bread and eggs, with which they feast in the evening, the youths being afterwards admitted to dance Horos with them.

These Lazarki dances clearly belong to the spring cycle of pre-Christian good-luck and fertility customs.

MUSIC

Antiphonal singing is a feature of some of the women's Horos. In some villages two sing the theme and are answered by another two. Again, in the South-West, one will sing the air, two others keeping up a peculiar drone to be answered by another group of three in the same manner. They sing and dance thus for hours.

Very interesting also are the pentatonic melodies which belong to an ancient and fast-disappearing style of singing and are used in some of the Ugârchin Horos-promenades.

Instruments are now replacing song. We use the bagpipe, the *kaval* (a type of flute) and the *dvoyanka* (double flute), also the *gadulka* (rebec) and the *tambura* (a mandoline type of instrument). The drum alone is also used for dancing. The players, who are frequently gypsies, will interpolate a sung verse or two. Young men returning from military service are introducing wind instruments and brass which they have played in military bands; thus every village in northern Bulgaria has now its small brass band, while the violin, brought in by gypsies in the days of Turkish occupation, has become a widespread folk instrument.

The most widely distributed Horo rhythm is 2/4 in moderate or very quick tempo, but 3/8 is also known. The most characteristic of Bulgarian dance rhythms are those called 'Bulgarian' by the Hungarian musician Béla Bartók. These rhythms are obtained from the combination of a dotted note, generally a dotted quaver (♪. = ♫♪ not being a triplet), with an undotted quaver (♪ = ♫). For example the Paidushka Horo rhythm is 5/16 in two beats, the second beat lengthened, i.e. ♪ ♪. = ♫ ♫♪. (Count an even 1-2, 1-2-3.) The Răchenitsa 7/16 rhythm is obtained from two undotted and one dotted quaver, i.e. ♪ ♪ ♪. = ♫ ♫ ♫♪. (Count an even 1-2, 1-2, 1-2-3 until familiar with the tune.) A whole series of dances are danced to mixed rhythms:

$$\frac{7+7}{16} + \frac{5+5}{16}; \frac{9}{16} + \frac{5+5}{16}; \frac{11}{16} + \frac{5+5}{16}; \frac{15}{16} + \frac{9}{16},$$

and so on.

COSTUME

Everything worn by both men and women is of home-made material.

There are three types of women's dress. The two-apron type shows a back and front apron instead of a skirt; the front one is red with geometrical patterns in light colours, the back one is gathered and embroidered but also in dark colours. A sleeveless bolero is worn over the chemise, and in winter a sheepskin or long white homespun coat.

The Sukman costume consists of a long skirt with an overdress below the knees, with or without sleeves; the Saya costume shows a *saya* or over-garment open all the way down, the skirts of which are open or crossed or just meet, with an apron over them.

Aprons show the Bulgarian woman's skill and artistic taste in their ornamentation.

Headgear is usually a kerchief of light cotton, silk or wool. It is folded diagonally, and the ends may hang down or be tied at the back or on the top of the head. Certain costumes demand a tiny hat to which the kerchief is artistically fastened, but in many districts only the married women cover their heads. Today head-dresses are kept for high days and holidays.

Men's costumes fall roughly into two categories, the white and the black. The first is found in the West as far as the River Iskâr. Its characteristics are tight white trousers and a shirt front with much or little embroidery. The coat is sometimes dark blue embroidered with white, sometimes white decorated with black braid, sleeveless and long-skirted. The belt is worn under the blue coat, over the white one. In winter sheepskin coats are worn with the wool inside, the skin embroidered and decorated with leather appliqué and embroidery. The white costume has several variants.

The black costume, made from the natural dark wool of the black sheep, has trousers tight up to the knees and bulky with heavy folds from the knees upwards. They are called *poturi*. A fawn or coloured waistcoat is covered by a black or red one, and a coat goes over all. Black leggings, bound on with black string, and a long hooded cloak give warmth in winter. A fur cap is worn with both black and white costumes.

Footgear for both men and women are *tsarvuli* made of hide, bound to the feet with string.

Regional costumes today are very expensive, and this is one of the main reasons for their sadly increasing disuse; in some places they are worn only on Sundays and in many have been completely abandoned. In the dance we notice free movements with the two-apron style, the pleated back apron swinging out very effectively, while the Thracian woman in her ground-length garments dances more gently.

FESTIVALS WHEN DANCING MAY BE SEEN

Winter:
Christmas,
Jan. 7th and 8th
Christmas singers with dances in Suhodol, Vrabnitsa and other villages in the Sofia district; Provadiya district.

January 13th
Suruvakari Carnival in Breznik and Radomir districts.

February 17th,
St. Trifon's Day
Masks and disguises, processions, Hobby Horses, dances.

Spring:
Carnival
The Kukeri appear in Elhovo district, foothills of Strandja mountains, districts of Aitos and Karlovo and other places.

Saturday before
Palm Sunday
Lazarki: girls visit houses with dances and singing in Dragalevtsi and other villages of Sofia district; Pomorie district.

June 3rd
Nestinari: fire dances with processions.

Summer
Fairs all over Bulgaria.

Autumn
Camel (Hobby Horse) at threshing time, district of Elhovo.

FOLK DANCE GROUPS

Groups of dancers are to be found in the towns of Nevrokop, Silistra, Pazardjik, Dobrich and Varna, and in the villages of Hlevene, Ugărchin, Boril and Bregovo.

In Sofia there are folk-dance groups of Municipal functionaries, of Post and Telegraph employees, of electrical workers, and many others.

The National Opera, the Military Music organisation and the National Militia have folk-dance groups.

The National Museum of Ethnology in Sofia (Section of Folk Music and Dance) gives information about folk festivals, fairs and dances. The Museum holds a collection of over 30,000 folk tunes.

The service in charge of 'self-expression' groups, the Committee for Science, Arts and Culture, has a special folklore section.

THE DANCES

TECHNICAL EDITORS
MURIEL WEBSTER AND KATHLEEN P. TUCK

ABBREVIATIONS

USED IN DESCRIPTION OF STEPS AND DANCES

r—right ⎱ referring to   R—right ⎱ describing turns or
l—left ⎰ hand, foot, etc. L—left ⎰ ground pattern
C—clockwise   C-C—counter-clockwise

For descriptions of foot positions and explanations of any ballet terms the following books are suggested for reference:

A Primer of Classical Ballet (Cecchetti method). Cyril Beaumont.

First Steps (R.A.D.). Ruth French and Felix Demery.

The Ballet Lover's Pocket Book. Kay Ambrose.

Reference books for description of figures:

The Scottish Country Dance Society's Publications. Many volumes, from Thornhill, Cairnmuir Road, Edinburgh 12.

The English Folk Dance and Song Society's Publications. Cecil Sharp House, 2 Regent's Park Road, London, N.W.1.

The Country Dance Book I–VI. Cecil J. Sharp. Novello & Co., London.

POISE OF BODY AND ARM HOLDS

The body and head should be held erect with the dignity so characteristic of the Bulgarian peasant. Many of the dances work up from a slow to a very lively rhythm, so that the chief requirement is light-footedness; but whatever the speed, that dignity must be preserved. This applies specially to the women, whose movements must be restrained while the men improvise leaps and stamps. Usually the body moves in one piece, turning to the R or to the L, but in a few dances there is a slight inclination of the upper part of the body.

The hands can be held naturally to the sides or placed on the hips. If a belt is worn this may be grasped in the front, at the side or behind. The hands may also be held forward at shoulder level, or raised above the head with a sharp or an obtuse elbow angle.

In the Horos (chain or circle dances) the hands may be joined in the following ways:—

(1) With the hands raised above the head.

(2) To form a double ring—one dancer passing his hands over those of his neighbour's, whose hands are below, and so on.

(3) The hands in shoulder grasp, or clasped so that they lie behind the head of the dancer on either side.

(4) The leader and the end dancer wave their free hand or a kerchief.

(5) In southern Bulgaria the hands are held at shoulder level, with the palms turned inward, and the elbows bent so that the shoulders of the dancers are more or less touching, and the grasp is made only by the middle fingers.

BASIC STEPS

These include walking, jumps, hops and pivots, which can be danced on the toes or the heels or on the whole foot. The steps can be small or large according to the speed of the music, and many of them can be taken either forward or backward or to the side.

Please read Music section pages 14-15 and carefully practise counting beats before trying these steps.

Swing Step (as in 'Temenugo, temenushke').

Step in any direction indicated and swing the free foot forward (or backward if indicated).

Hopping Swing Step (as in 'Tsone, milo chedo').

While hopping 3 times on the l foot, swing the r knee in front and across to the L, then sideways to the R, then forward to step on this foot. (Counted Slow, Slow, Quick, Slow.) The step can be repeated with the l foot.

Steps for use in Răchenitsa (7/16).

In order to capture the rhythm, the following steps should be practised, counting 1–2, 1–2, 1–2–3 (see page 15), gradually accelerating until the desired speed is reached. The basic step is a form of Pas de Basque with a prolonged 3rd beat.

A. STEPS DANCED MORE OR LESS ON THE SPOT

	Beats
1 *Pas de Basque* (7/16 time signature).	
Spring on to heel of r foot.	1–2
Place l toe close to r foot, momentarily changing the weight.	3–4
Spring again on to whole of r foot.	5–6–7
This step can be taken also on the l foot.	
2 *Toe-Balance Step*	
Step forward in front of l foot on toes of r foot.	1–2
Replace weight on to l foot (up on toes).	3–4

Bring r foot backward to side of l foot, still on toes. This step can be repeated with the l foot.	5–6–7

3 *Spring-Stamp Step*
Step to R with r foot.	1–2
Close l foot to side of r foot.	3–4
Spring, to land on toes with both feet together, and quickly change to a stamp on the heels.	5–6–7

4 *Hop-Stamp Step*
Hop on l foot, with r knee bent and raised forward; then quickly stamp with the r foot in place.	1 2
Change weight on to toes of l foot.	3–4
Change weight on to toes of r foot.	5–6–7
Repeat by hopping on r foot, and so on. *N.B.*—This step can be taken forward, backward or sideways.	

B. MOVING FORWARD

5 *Leaping Step*
Small leap forward on to r foot.	1–2
Close l foot to r foot on toes.	3–4
r foot forward on toes, transferring weight.	5–6–7
(Rather like a triple run.)	

6 *Hop-Swing Step*
Small hop forward on r foot.	1–2
Swing l leg forward.	3–4
Step forward on toes of l foot.	5–6–7

7 *Hop-Toe Step*
Small hop forward on l foot.	1–2
Step forward on toes of r foot.	3–4
Step forward on toes of l foot.	5–6–7

Repeat again with l foot, and so on.
N.B.—This step can be danced with the r foot and can be taken moving obliquely to the R or L, or backward.

C. MOVING BACKWARD

(See also Steps 4 and 7, each of which can be taken moving backward.)

8 *Change Step*
Step back on to toes of r foot.	1–2
Step back on to toes of l foot, to side of r foot.	3–4
Step back on to toes of r foot.	5–6–7
Repeat by stepping back on to l foot, etc.	

9 *Hop-Swing Step*
Hop backward on to r foot.	1–2
Swing l foot across in front of r foot.	3–4
Step on to toes of l foot.	5–6–7
Repeat by hopping backward on to l foot.	

D. MOVING SIDEWAYS

10 *Toe-Heel Pivot Step*
Pivot on toes of both feet, so that heels are turned to R.	1–2
Take weight on to both heels.	3–4
Pivot on heels, so that toes of both feet face to R.	5–6–7
Repeat these movements twice (2 bars).	
Stamp on both heels.	1 and 2
Hold.	3–4
Repeat stamp on both heels.	5–6–7
(The whole of this step-phrase takes 4 bars of music.)	

RĂCHENITSA

Region — All over Bulgaria. (The costumes shown in Plate 4 are those of Vidin.)

Character — Energetic, with a gradual increase in tempo until at the end the dancers are somewhat dazed.

Formation — Essentially a couple dance (see the account on p. 9). This dance is based on numerous fundamental figures described in general terms unhampered by rules. The dancers improvise on these as they are carried away by the rhythm. The men follow their inspiration, so that each dancer is in fact dancing a solo. For detailed descriptions of steps see Basic Steps, pp. 21–23. The hands are used freely to emphasise the movements.

Dance

MUSIC
Bars

FIGURE I

The first dancer advances to the centre of the dance-space with Step 5. He (or she) is followed a little later by his (or her) partner. They dance independently round the dance-space, to end facing each other about two yards apart.

Tune I
1–16

FIGURE II

Advance towards each other with 4 steps— the woman No. 7 or 5, the man No. 6. Return

1–8

RĂCHENITSA

Arranged by Arnold Foster

1st Tune

Allegro ♪♪♩.= 60-72

to places with 4 steps, the woman No. 8, the man No. 9.

FIGURE III

Advance a few steps (No. 8), dance step No. 10, then return again to places.

9–16

FIGURE IV

The woman flees from her partner, circling and crossing the dance-space—first with her back to him, then facing him—to dance Steps No. 8 or No. 4, pivoting on herself with full circles and waving her kerchief.

Tune I
1–16
twice

Meanwhile the man draws the circle more closely round the woman, using Steps 6, 7 or 9, to end facing his partner while dancing the following step:
Spring into squatting position (knees fully bent and feet together), then jump to standing position, stretching one leg forward. Repeat the squatting and stretch the other leg forward. (These two steps take 2 bars of music.)

FIGURE V

The woman dances more or less on the spot, changing between steps No. 1 and 2 or 4 and 10. She raises the arms either forward or above her head, holding the ends of the kerchief in each hand and turning it in the rhythm of the dance; or she may hold her hands freely and make any gestures she feels appropriate.

1–16

The man continues his tricks, springing to a half-kneeling position, knocking the ground with the knee on which he is kneeling on beats

2nd Tune (begins at Figure IV)

1, 2 and 5, 6, 7 in the bar and turning it slightly inward. He then rises lightly and makes a few springs on both feet, then jumps to repeat a squatting step and the half-kneeling step on the other knee. He snaps his fingers all the time and calls softly

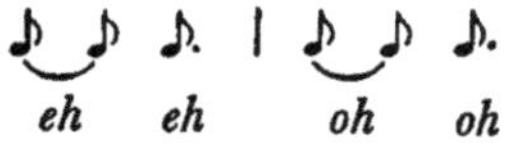

$$\flat \; \flat \; \flat. \; | \; \flat \; \flat \; \flat.$$
eh eh   oh oh

in time to the music.

FIGURE VI

The man repeats his steps, trying to excel still more in height and length, and when passing from one step to the other he shouts loudly. The woman dances on the spot with springs and pivots or uses Step 10; then, moving freely to make room for her partner's fiery dancing, she uses Step 5.

1–16

FIGURE VII

The woman gives her hands to the man. Having recognised each other's skill in the dance, they move together C-C round the dance-space at a very quick tempo, as in a chain dance. After once round they leave the floor. Towards the end of their dance other couples often join them.

1–16

If the Răchenitsa is danced by two men, they try to outdo each other in daredevil tricks.

Plate 3 'Violet, Little Violet'. Thrace

TSONE, MILO CHEDO

(*Tsone, dear child*)

Region	Zemen, Kyustendil district, and Dimitrovo (formerly Pernik).
Character	Beginning with a moderately quick, easy movement, increasing gradually, decreasing again, to end in a *prestissimo*.
Formation	For any number of dancers, men and women, standing one behind the other with hands on hips, facing C-C in a circle. A few dancers begin, and gradually others take their places behind them. Some carry a kerchief which they wave. The rebec player (*gadular*) stands in the centre of the circle. Towards the end all join hands in a chain, the dance ending in a Horo in very quick tempo accompanied by a song or a drum.

Dance

The 14/16 rhythm is beaten in four, i.e. 1–2, 1–2, 1, 1–2, and counted s., s., Q., s. The body is turned slightly (not more than 45°) to the R or to the L in the direction of the swinging foot. The man can take the raised foot behind the other in the Swing step.	MUSIC *Bars*
FIGURE I. Moving forward C-C.	
1 Three hopping steps on l foot, swinging the r knee in front and across to the L, out to the R side and straight forward, to step forward on this foot. (Counted s., s., Q., and s. for the step forward.)	1

TSONE, MILO CHEDO

2 Repeat movements of bar 1, but the hops are taken on the r foot, and so on.	2
3 Repeat movements of bars 1 and 2. The man's step is slightly different from the woman's—on the first two hops he swings the r foot across behind the l, so that the r knee faces to the R and the heel to the L.	3–4

FIGURE II: HORO (Chain Dance). Moving C-C.
The joined hands are held about shoulder level, with the elbows bent, and are swung in rhythm.

1 Step on r foot to R (s.). Step on l foot in front of r foot, to R (s.). Spring on to r foot to R with an inward pivot of the r foot, so that the body faces slightly L (Q.). Step on l foot behind r foot and to R (s.).	1
2 Step on r foot to R (s.). Swing l foot across r (s.). Spring on to l foot with a slight inward pivot of the foot (Q.). Step r foot behind l foot to L (s.).	2
3 Step on l foot to L (s.). Swing r foot across l foot (s.). Spring on r foot to R with an inward pivot of this foot (Q.). Step on to l foot behind r foot to R (s.).	3
Repeat movements of bars 1–3, beginning on bar 4.	4
Repeat whole dance, or Horo only, as often as wished, ending prestissimo.	

In this chain dance the dance phrases do not correspond to the musical phrases; therefore begin repeats without reference to the bar number.

TEMENUGO, TEMENUSHKE

(Violet, Little Violet)

Region   Thrace: district of Haskovo.

Character   Quiet at first, gradually increasing then decreasing in speed.

Formation   Chain or circle with ordinary chain grasp. On the forward steps the hands are tossed forward and upward and the circle draws in; on the backward steps the circle is opened again. The forward steps are longer than the backward ones, so that the chain progresses slowly to the R.

Dance	MUSIC Bars
FIGURE I	
a Start with toes to centre and move C.-C.	1
Step obliquely forward on r foot (Quick).	(beat 1)
Step obliquely forward on l foot (Quick).	(beat 2)
Step obliquely forward on r, swinging l foot forward (Slow).	2 (beats 1–2)
Step obliquely forward on l, swinging r foot forward (Slow).	3 (beats 1–2)
b Moving backward to L, C.	4
Step obliquely backward on r foot (Q.).	(beat 1)
Step obliquely backward on l foot (Q.).	(beat 2)
Step obliquely backward on r foot, swinging l foot forward and across r (s.).	5 (beats 1–2)
Step obliquely backward on l foot, swinging r foot forward across l (s.).	6 (beats 1–2)

TEMENUGO, TEMENUSHKE

FIGURE II

a Moving C-C. | 7
Step forward obliquely on to r foot (Q.). | (beat 1)
Step forward obliquely on to l foot (Q.). | (beat 2)
Repeat movements of bar 7 (Q., Q.). | 8
Step forward on to r, swinging the l leg forward or stamping on the l heel after a short brush of the foot. | 9 (beats 1–2)

b Moving backward but still C-C. | 10
Step back on to l foot behind r foot to R. | (beat 1)
Step back on to r foot with a slight inward pivot of the foot. | (beat 2)
Repeat movements of bar 10. | 11
Step back on l foot and stamp r heel after a slight brush of this foot and slight pivot of the l foot. | 12 (beats 1–2)

FIGURE I (SECOND TIME) begins on bar 13. The steps will then come on the beats but not in the bars given above. Counting should therefore be continued until the steps are automatic. If the dance is performed four times and the music three times both will end simultaneously.

Frequently—as in this dance—the dance phrase and the musical phrase do not synchronise. However, the rhythm of the steps is so strong that it counteracts this discrepancy.

'*Violet, little Violet,*
Whom love you, whom trick you?'

'*I love a brown shepherd lad—*
A brown shepherd, my brown Ivan,
Who turns twisted distaffs,
Twisted distaffs and kavali [flutes].

'*He has made me a distaff*
And carved himself upon it,
That I may see him when I spin.

'*He has made himself a kaval*
And upon it has he carved me,
When he plays it for to see me.'

OVCHATA

(The Sheep's Dance)

Region The village of Hlevene, in the Lovech district.

Character Moderately fast, even but energetic, with a slight increase in speed and with clear stamping at the end of every figure.

Formation A straight line of 10–20 dancers standing alternately man and woman. Two lines may dance at the same time, standing facing each other.

Dance	MUSIC Bars
The short linked line moves in a small space to the L and R with running, swinging and stamping steps. The dancers' arms are crossed alternately in front of and behind those of the next dancer, the hands holding the top edge of the next dancer's belt.	

FIGURE I

Start with feet together, toes to centre.
Step on r foot to R (Q.).   1
Swing l foot across r foot (Q.).
Step on l foot to L (Q.).   2
Swing r foot across l foot (Q.).
Step on r foot to R (Q.).   3
Beat with l foot, close to but in front of r foot (Q.).
Repeat beat with l, but do not take weight on to this foot (s.).   4

OVCHATA

Arranged by Arnold Foster

FIGURE II
Step on l foot to L (Q.).	5
Swing r foot across l foot (Q.).	
Step on r foot to R (Q.).	6
Swing l foot across r foot (Q.).	
Step on l foot to L (Q.).	7
Beat with r foot, close to and in front of l foot (Q.).	
Repeat beat with l foot without taking the weight on to this foot (s.).	8

FIGURE III (Running steps to R)
Step sideways on r foot (Q.).	9
Step sideways on l foot crossed behind r (Q.).	
Step sideways on r foot (Q.).	10
Step sideways on l foot crossed in front of r foot (Q.).	
Step sideways on r foot (Q.).	11
Beat with l foot close to and in front of r foot (Q.).	
Repeat beat without taking weight on to l foot (s.).	12

FIGURE IV
Repeat movements of Figure II.	13–16

FIGURE V
Repeat movements of Figure I.	17–20

FIGURE VI (Running steps to L)
Repeat movements of Figure III, starting with l foot and moving to the L.	21–24

This dance is accompanied by a shepherd's pipe.

Plate 4
Rǎchenitsa

BIBLIOGRAPHY

ARNAUDOV, M.—'Le Carneval et les Rosalies.' ('Kukeri i Rusalii.' *Sbornik za Narodni Umotvoreniya*, vol. XXXIV. Sofia, 1920.

BUKORESHLIEV, A., V. STOIN and R. KATSAROVA.—'Folk Songs of th Rhodopes.' *Sbornik za Narodni Umotvoreniya*, vol. XXXIX. 1934 (In Bulgarian.)

DJOUDJEFF, STOYAN.—*Rythme et mesure dans la musique populaire bulgare* Paris, 1931.

—— *Bulgarian Folk Dances*. Sofia, 1946. (In Bulgarian.)

HRISTOV, D.—'The Rhythmic Bases of Bulgarian Folk Music.' *Sborni* *za Narodni Umotvoreniya*, vol. XXVII. 1913. (In Bulgarian.)

KATSAROVA-KUKUDOVA, R.—*Bulgarische Tänze und Tanzrhythmen* Berlin, 1942.

KATSAROVA, R.—'Lazarnica.' *Journal of the English Folk Dance an Song Society*, vol. II. 1935.

KUKUDOV, S.—'Několik poznamek o bulharském lidovém tanci. *Tanečni List*. Prague, 1948.

STOIN, VASILI.—*Folk Songs of the Central Region of North Bulgaria*. Sofia, 1931. (In Bulgarian.)

—— *Bulgarian Folk Songs of Eastern and Western Thrace*. Sofia, 1939 (In Bulgarian.)

TSONEV, B.—'Danses populaires bulgares.' *Revue Médico-Pédagogique* 1941.

VAKARELSKI, HRISTO.—*Bulgarian National Costumes*. Sofia, 1942. (In Bulgarian.)

Bulgarian Folk Dances. A handbook for teachers of physical training, published by the Ministry of Public Education. Sofia, 1946. (In Bulgarian.)

FILMS: *Bulgarian Folk Dances* and *Bulgarian Wedding*. Obtainable from 'Bâlgarska Kinematografia', Sofia.

www.ingramcontent.com/pod-product-compliance
Lightning Source LLC
Chambersburg PA
CBHW061743290426
43661CB00127B/964